Log Cabin Kitty

WRITTEN BY
Donna Rubin

ILLLUSTRATED BY
Susan J. Halbower

TCU Press
Fort Worth, Texas

Library of Congress Cataloging-in-Publication Data

Rubin, Donna.
  Log cabin kitty / written by Donna Rubin ; illlustrated by Susan J. Halbower.
      p. cm.
  Summary: "Log cabin kitty" is a tour of original log houses reassembled and preserved at Log Cabin
Village in Fort Worth, Texas, narrated by a fictional version of a real cat that once lived at the village.
The site includes 14 historical structures including a working blacksmith shop and the Parker Cabin,
where Cynthia Ann Parker spent time after she was returned from her Native American abductors.
The narrative includes information about domestic pioneer life, recipes, and a glossary of terms.
  Audience: K through Grade 3.
  1. Log Cabin Village (Fort Worth, Tex.)--Juvenile literature. 2. Log cabins--Texas--Fort Worth--
Juvenile literature. 3. Historic house museums--Texas--Fort Worth--Juvenile literature. 4. Frontier and
pioneer life--Texas--19th century--Juvenile literature. 5. Texas--Social life and customs--19th century--
Juvenile literature. I. Halbower, Susan J. II. Title.
F394.F7R83 2012
976.4'5315--dc23
                                2012029402

TCU Press
P.O. Box 298300
Fort Worth, Texas 76129
817.257.7822
www.prs.tcu.edu

To order books call 1.800.826.8911

To my loving husband and family for their
endless support and pioneer spirit.
- DPR

For my pioneer ancestors who paved the way,
and mother, who set a fearless example
- SJH

LOG CABIN VILLAGE

Shaw Gristmill

Herb

Blacksmith

Tompkins

Parker

Smokehouse

Marine Schoolhouse

Kitty

Howard

Foster

Pickard

Seela

FORT WORTH TEXAS

I'm the Log Cabin Kitty
And I'm sittin' mighty pretty.
I live in a village from a long time ago.

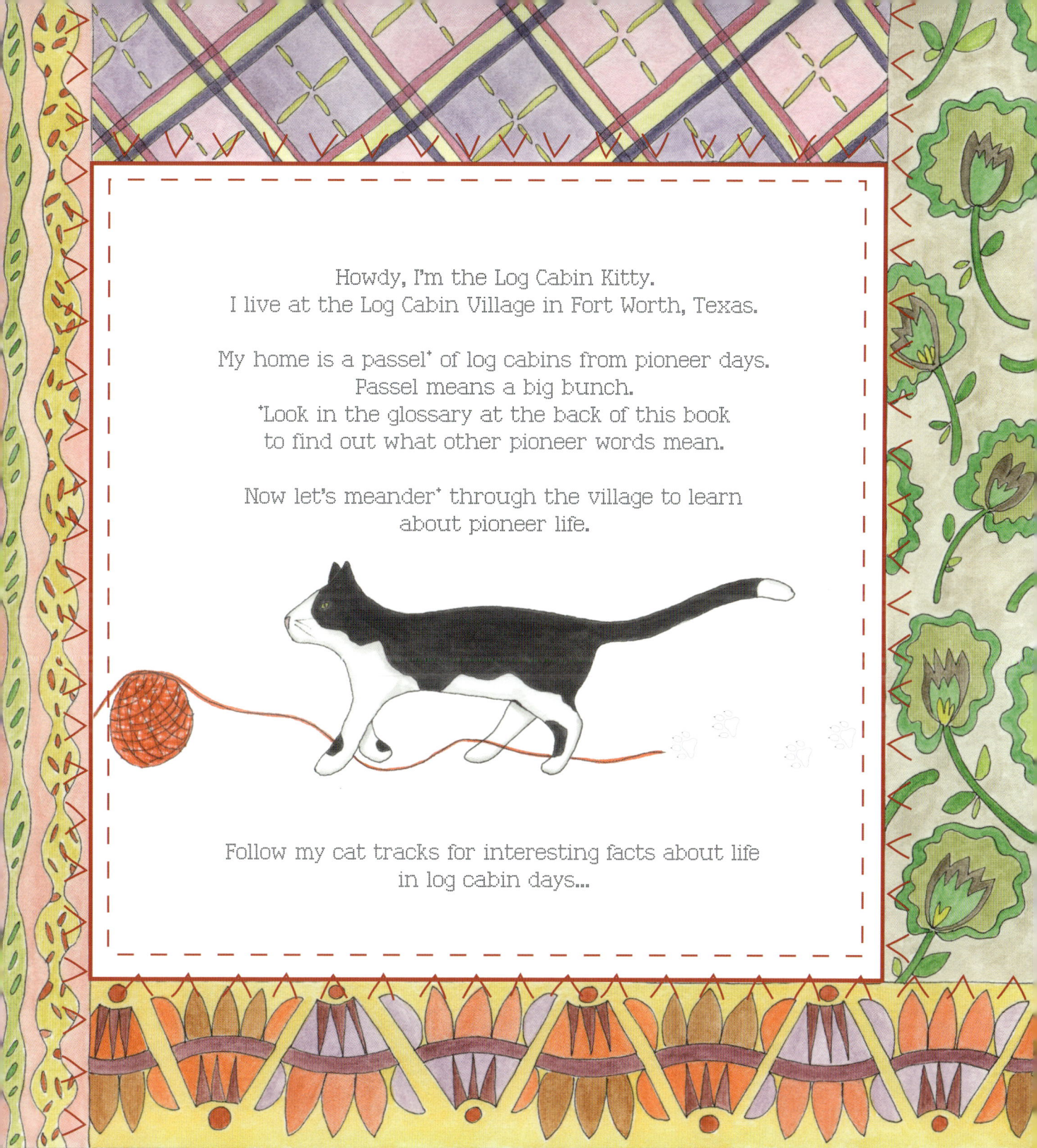

Howdy, I'm the Log Cabin Kitty.
I live at the Log Cabin Village in Fort Worth, Texas.

My home is a passel* of log cabins from pioneer days.
Passel means a big bunch.
*Look in the glossary at the back of this book
to find out what other pioneer words mean.

Now let's meander* through the village to learn
about pioneer life.

Follow my cat tracks for interesting facts about life
in log cabin days...

First, we'll mosey* into the Foster cabin.
This eight-room home was said to be one
of the finest log houses in Texas back in 1858.

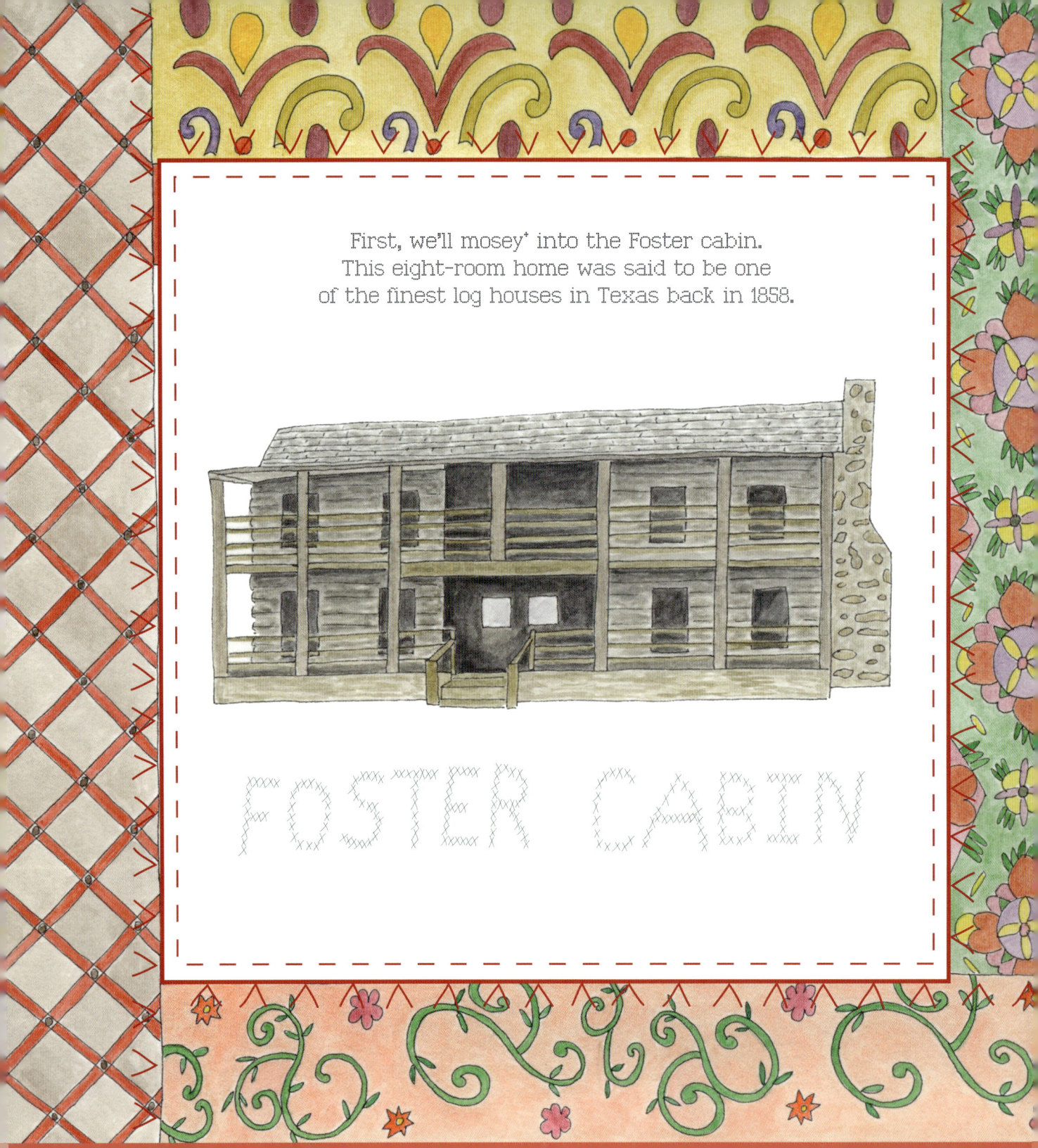

FOSTER CABIN

Like all the cabins in the village,
the Foster cabin was moved log-by-log
and reassembled to look just like the good ol' days.

CAT TRACK FACT:
Log houses were first built in the forests of Europe.
Swedish colonists built the earliest log homes in America
around 1630.

You can bet the Fosters were some pretty fancy folks having a two-story cabin with this fine piano and settee.[*]

I wish I could play a tune for you folks, but my paws are just too short.

I'm a music lovin' kitty—
Wish I could play a little ditty
On this old-time piano to give you folks a show.

CAT TRACK FACT:
Pioneers from miles around joined together for house
raisings to help each other build log homes on the frontier.

Hewn* logs were notched at the corners and chinked*
between cracks to make sturdy walls. The cabins had dirt or wooden
floors and stone fireplaces, and a window or two
if the owners could afford to have glass shipped to them
from the cities back East.

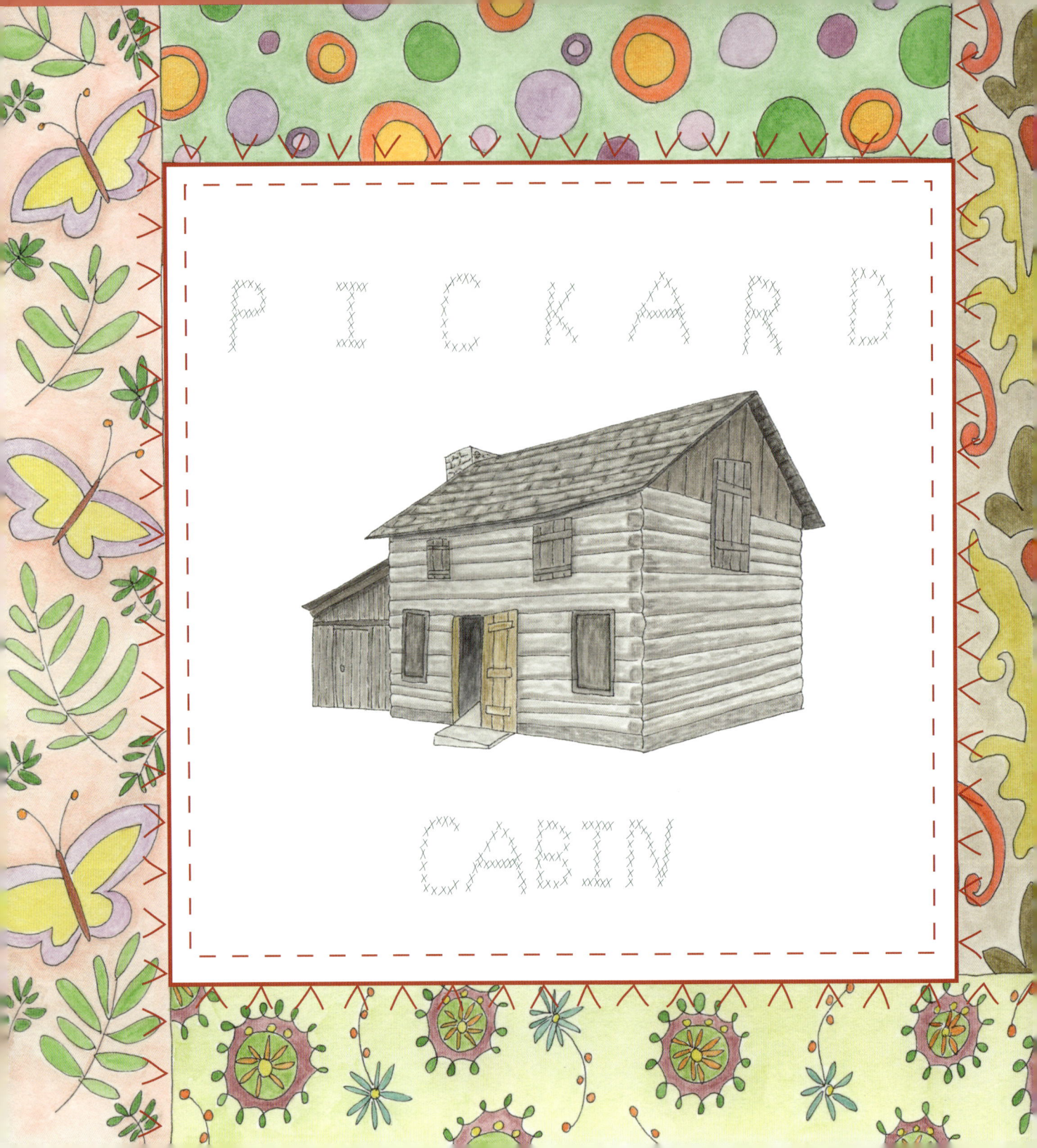

PICKARD

CABIN

Yonder* down the trail is the Pickard home. This cabin was built around 1850. The Pickards raised eight children in this one-room cabin with a sleeping loft.

Mr. and Mrs. Pickard worked from sunup to sundown just to feed and clothe their offspring.* You can bet those younguns had their share of chores to do, too. Everyone worked hard to make the things they needed in pioneer days.

I'm the Log Cabin Kitty
And I'm sittin' mighty pretty.
I live in a village from a long time ago.

CAT TRACK FACT:
Blankets were woven in jacquard* patterns on looms.

Quilts were pieced together by hand-stitching small pieces
of fabric scraps in patterns known as the wedding ring,
log cabin, and lone star, which are still popular today.

In the Isaac Seela cabin we see thread being
made on spinning wheels. Pioneer women
spent many back-breaking hours spinning
wool, cotton, or flax and weaving enough
yards of homespun* to outfit
a large pioneer family.

Pioneer kids were happy
to have one cotton outfit for the summer
and one woolen one for the winter,
no matter how scratchy those
long johns* felt.

CAT TRACK FACT:
Pioneers made the few clothes they owned from scratch.[*]
After gathering and cleaning the wool or cotton needed,
the women would spin the thread on spinning wheels.

I'm the spinning wheel kitty;
I like to spin and sew
And weave upon a loom to make a rug or throw.

CAT TRACK FACT:
The Great Walking Wheel was so named because a woman
had to walk many miles back and forth just to spin
enough thread for a simple shirt.

Next, the thread had to be woven into cloth,
and then the cloth was cut and sewn into clothing.

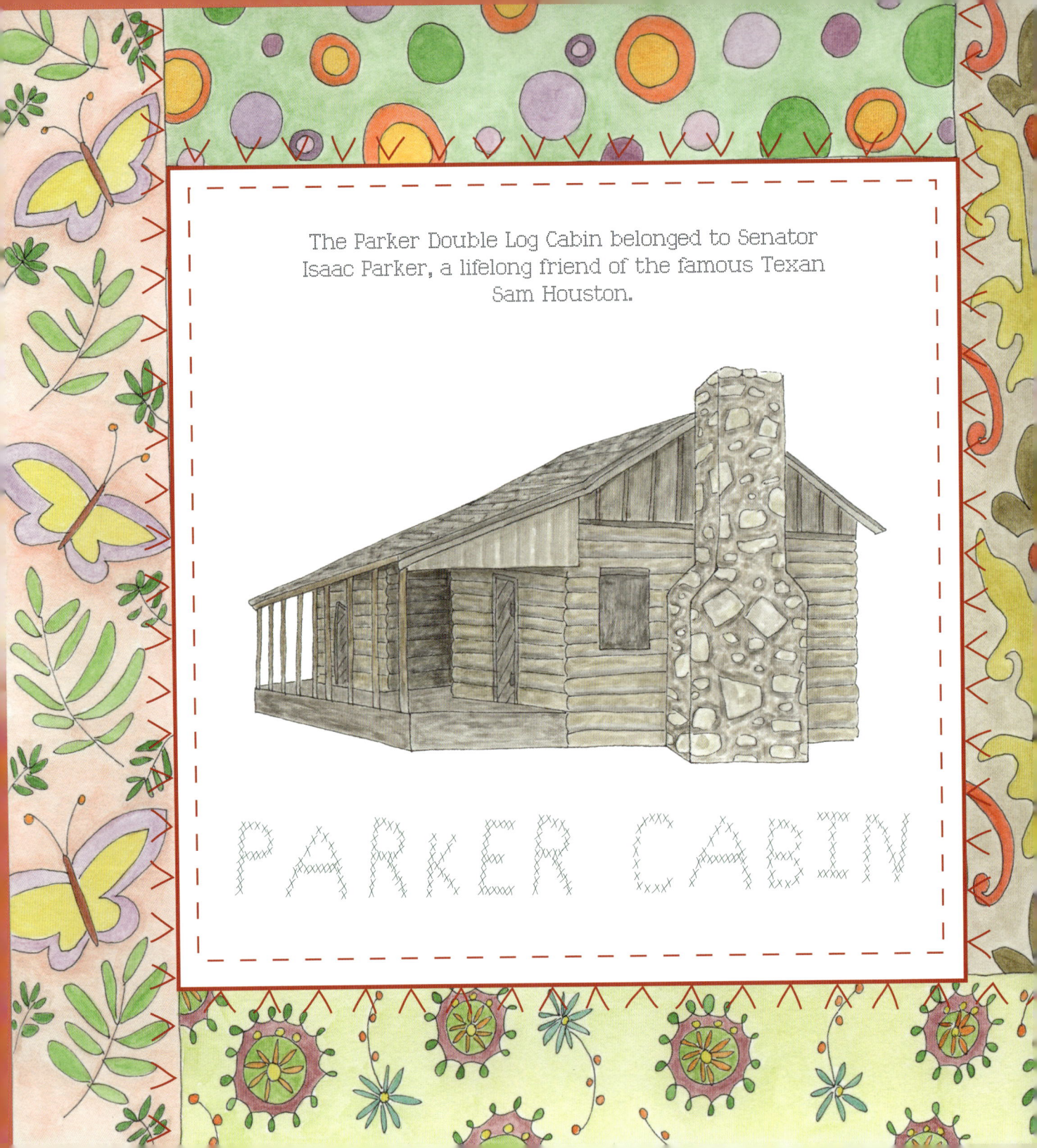

The Parker Double Log Cabin belonged to Senator
Isaac Parker, a lifelong friend of the famous Texan
Sam Houston.

PARKER CABIN

This very cabin is where Cynthia Ann Parker,
the senator's niece, lived after she was recaptured
from the Comanche Indians.

Cynthia Ann lived 25 years with the Indians, married
Chief Nocona, and gave birth to the last great
chief of the Comanche tribe, Quanah Parker.

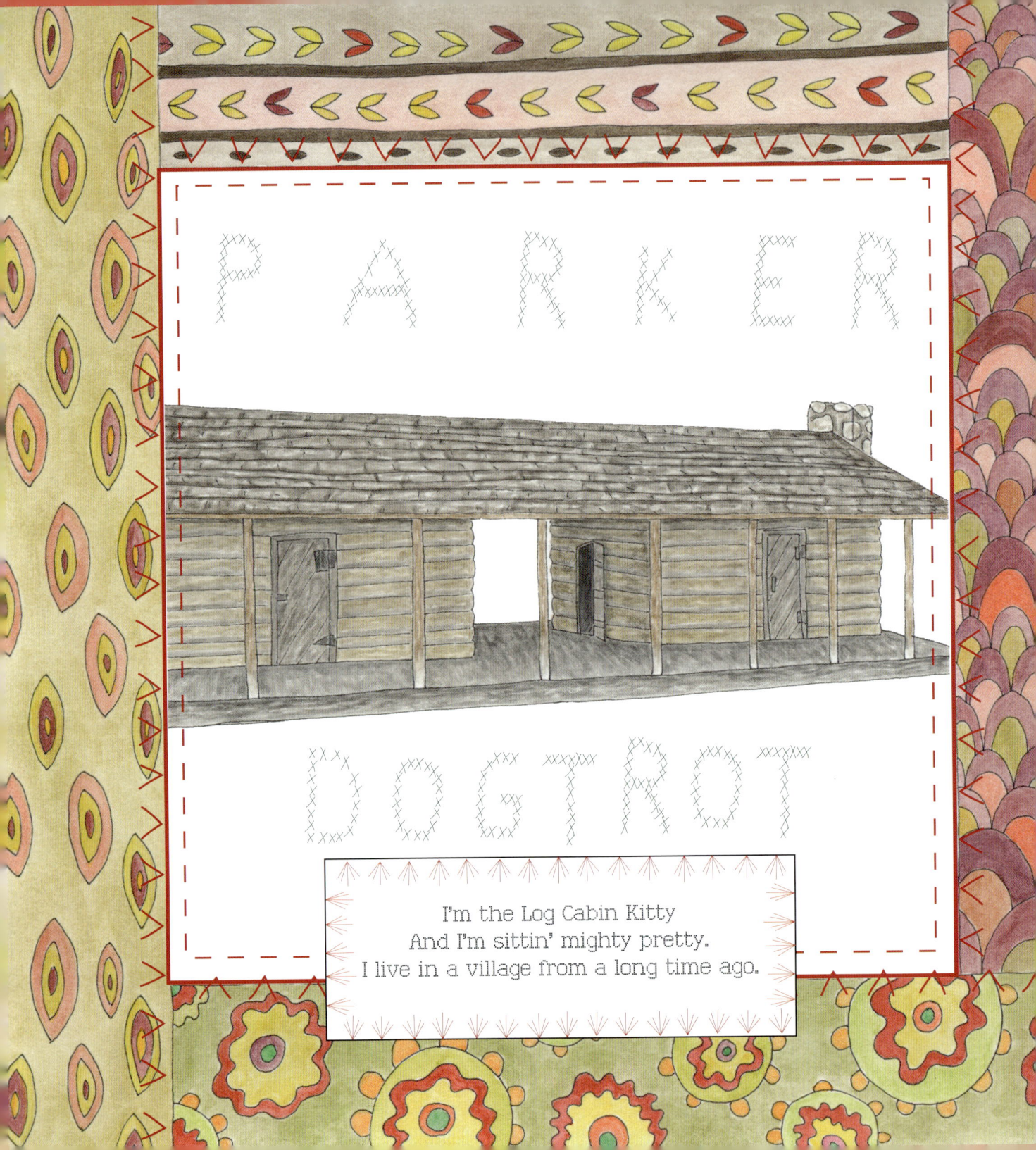

PARKER

DOGTROT

I'm the Log Cabin Kitty
And I'm sittin' mighty pretty.
I live in a village from a long time ago.

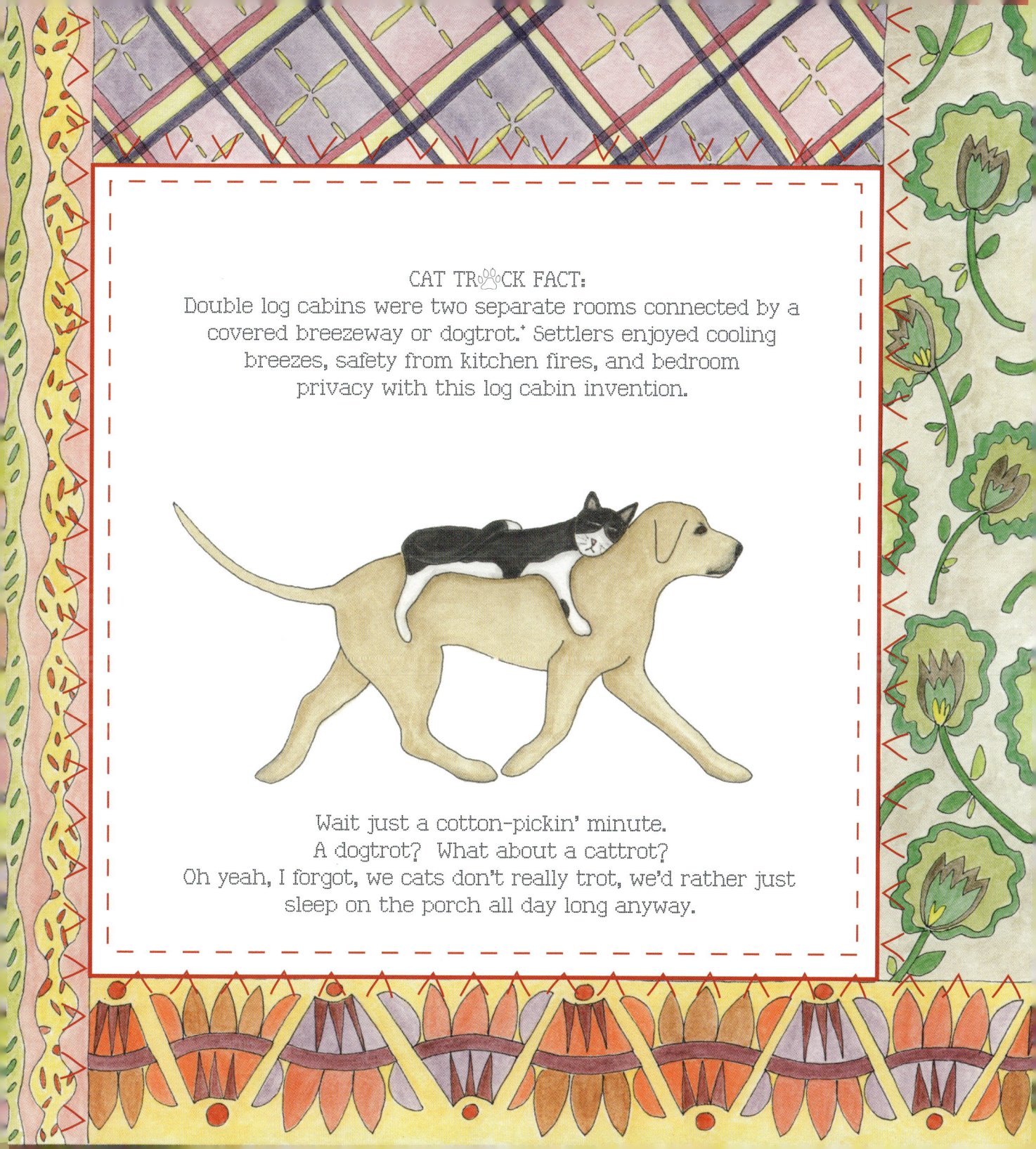

CAT TRACK FACT:
Double log cabins were two separate rooms connected by a covered breezeway or dogtrot.* Settlers enjoyed cooling breezes, safety from kitchen fires, and bedroom privacy with this log cabin invention.

Wait just a cotton-pickin' minute.
A dogtrot? What about a cattrot?
Oh yeah, I forgot, we cats don't really trot, we'd rather just sleep on the porch all day long anyway.

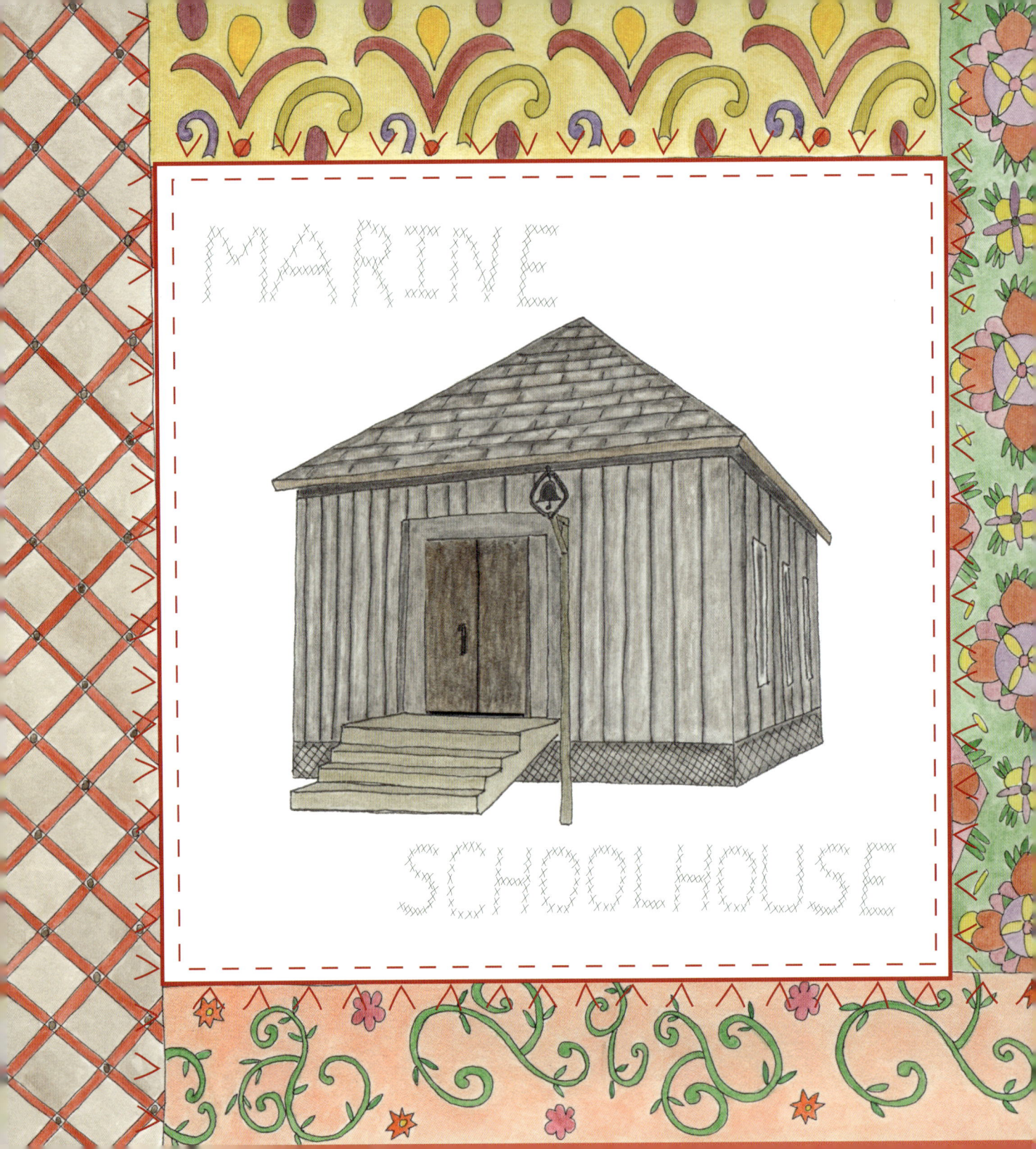

MARINE

SCHOOLHOUSE

At one end of our path is the Marine Schoolhouse,
the oldest one-room schoolhouse in Fort Worth, Texas.
Since 1872 youngsters have been learning the Three Rs—
readin', 'ritin', and 'rithmetic'—right here in this room.

Today you can come and wear old fashioned clothes,
sit on wooden benches, and eat your lunch from a tin pail
just like pioneer students from long ago.

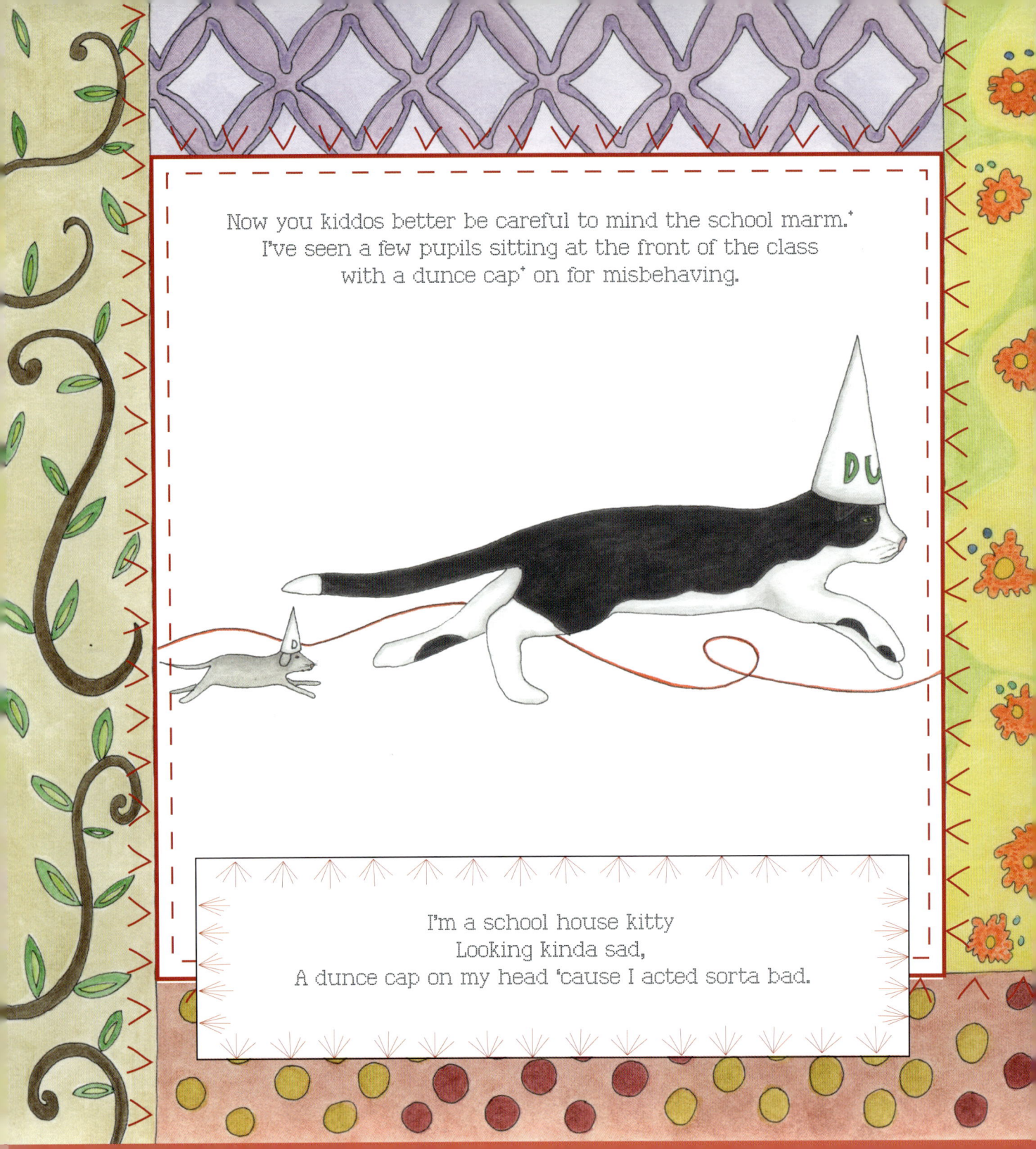

Now you kiddos better be careful to mind the school marm.*
I've seen a few pupils sitting at the front of the class
with a dunce cap* on for misbehaving.

I'm a school house kitty
Looking kinda sad,
A dunce cap on my head 'cause I acted sorta bad.

CAT TRACK FACT:
Back in the olden days students were expected to do chores
before they went to school every morning and after they
returned home in the evening. Pioneer children had to do
their ciphering* by the light of a fireplace after a long
day of learning at school and working on the farm.

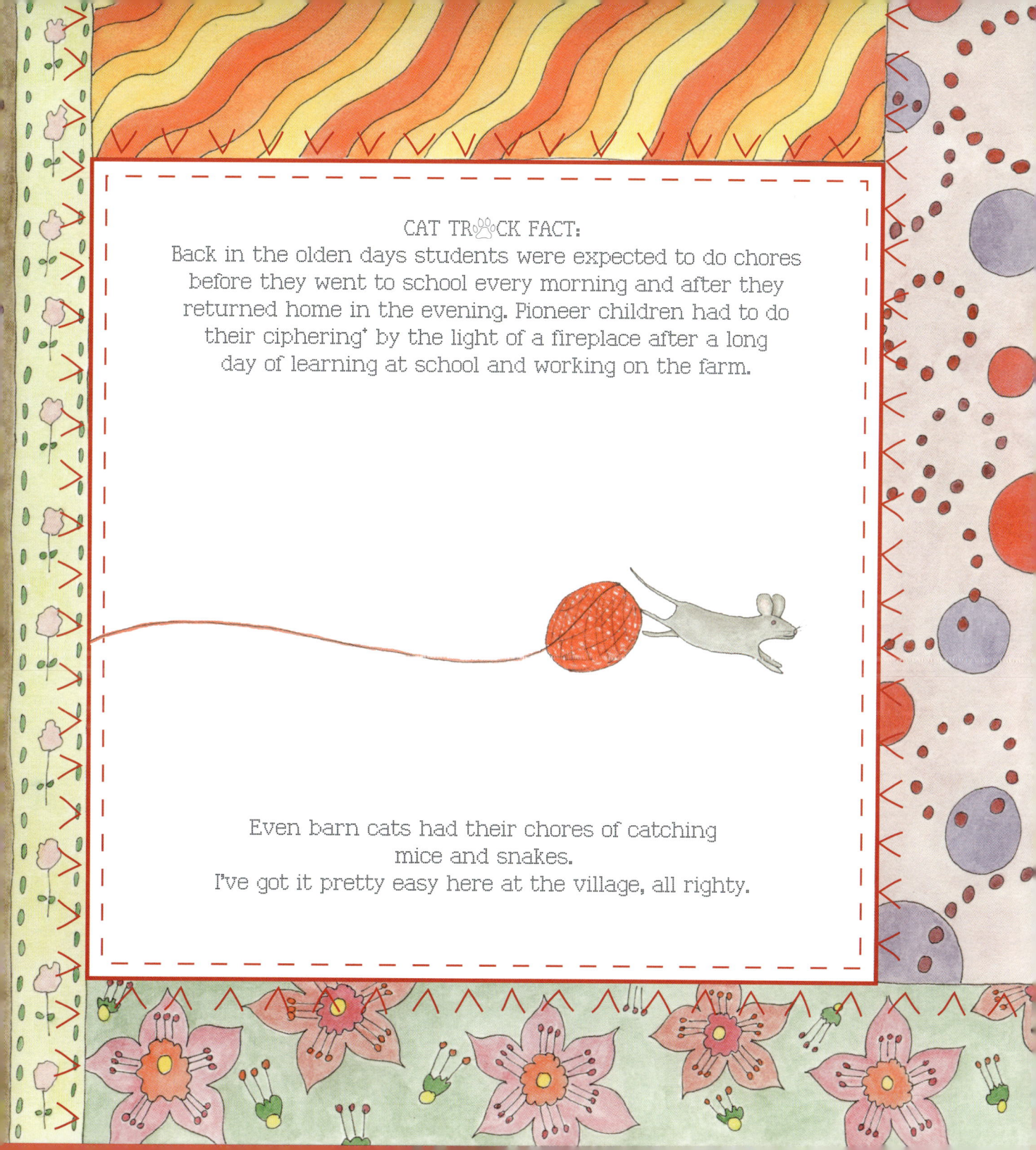

Even barn cats had their chores of catching
mice and snakes.
I've got it pretty easy here at the village, all righty.

KITTY CABIN

I'm the Log Cabin Kitty
And I'm sittin' mighty pretty.
I live in a village from a long time ago.

I reckon' I'm a right special cat around these parts 'cause
the fine folks at Log Cabin Village built me
a two-story kitty cabin.

THERE'S NO PLACE LIKE HOME.

Meow, wow. There's no place like home.

Around the corner lies the Hartsford Howard house, another two-story log cabin in the village. This 1858 cabin was built in an area that saw many conflicts with local Native American tribes. Sometimes farmers would trade or buy land cheaply from the Indians and turn around and sell it at a much higher price to pioneers wanting to settle in Texas.

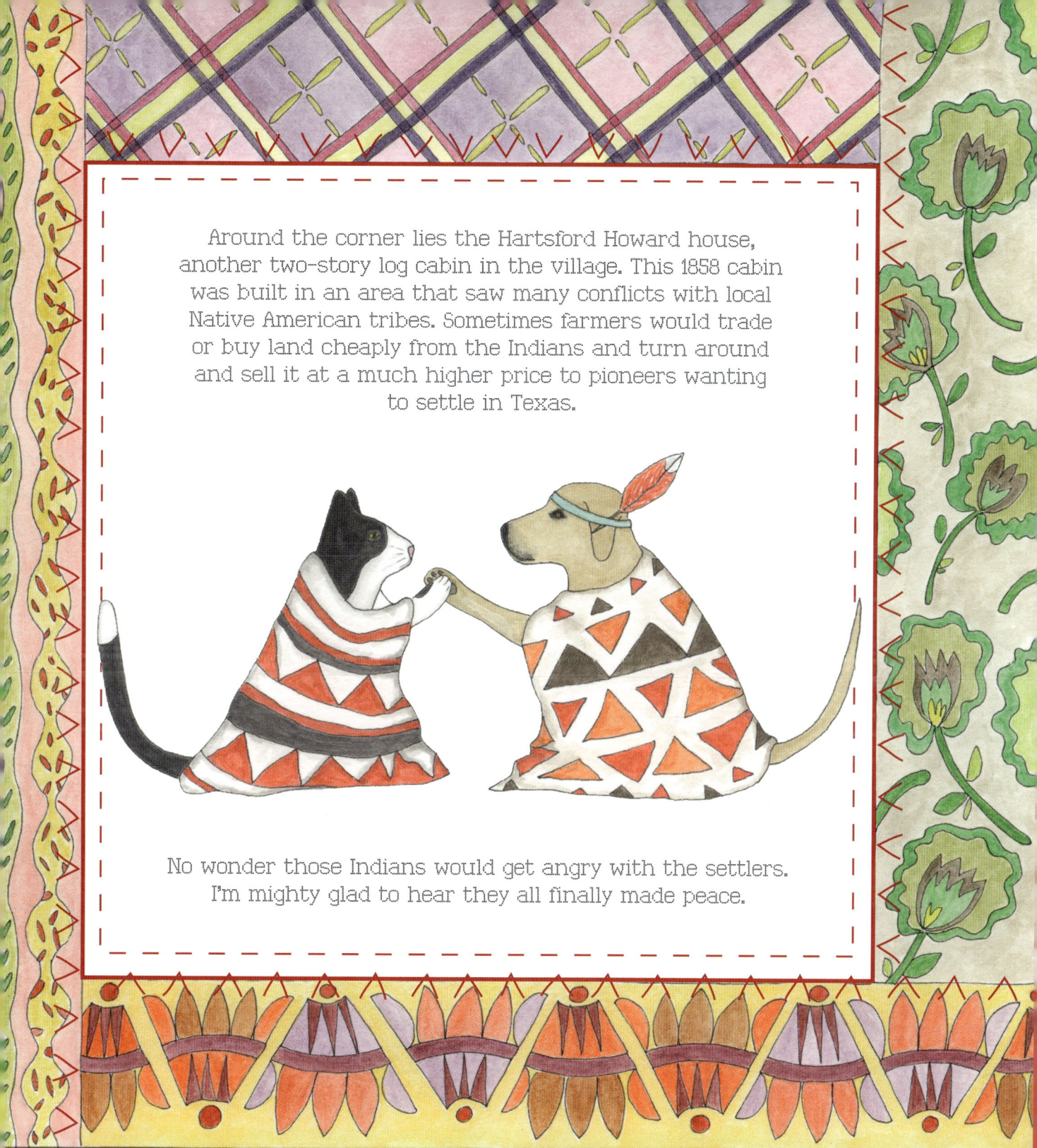

No wonder those Indians would get angry with the settlers. I'm mighty glad to hear they all finally made peace.

The Hartsford Howard was restored as
a woodwright's shop. It's amazing to see how beautiful
furniture was made with such primitive tools.

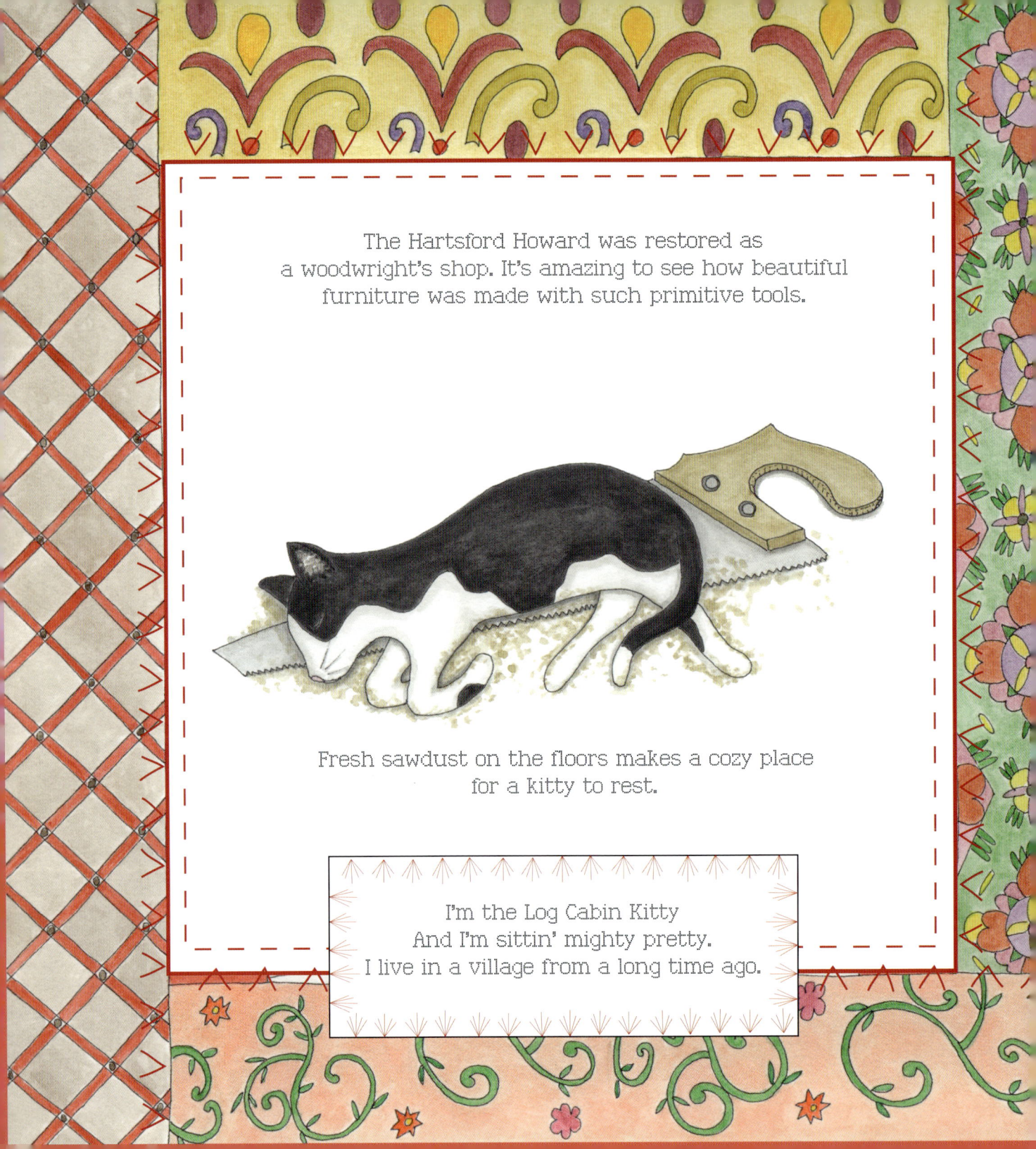

Fresh sawdust on the floors makes a cozy place
for a kitty to rest.

I'm the Log Cabin Kitty
And I'm sittin' mighty pretty.
I live in a village from a long time ago.

CAT TR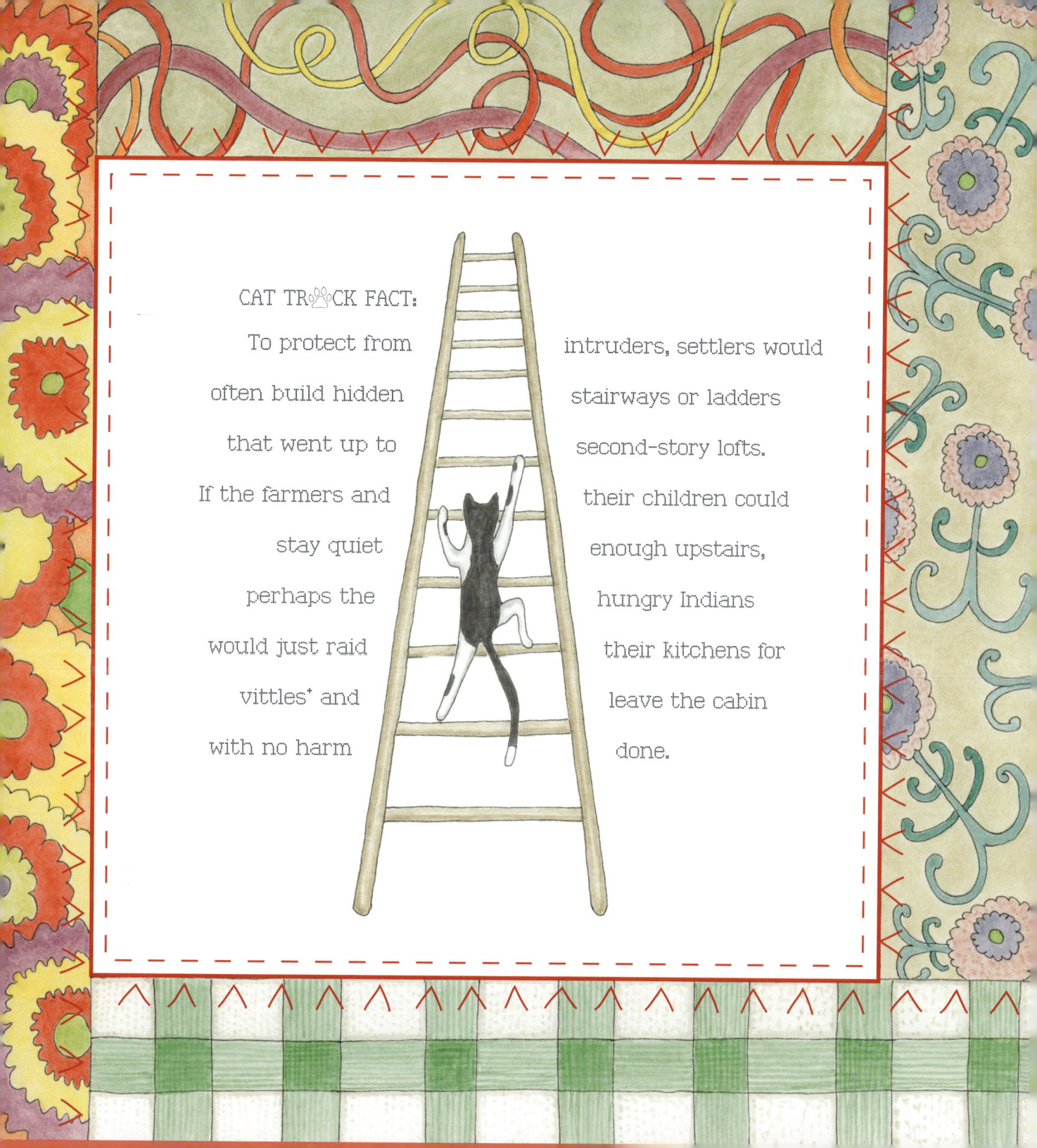CK FACT:

To protect from intruders, settlers would
often build hidden stairways or ladders
that went up to second-story lofts.
If the farmers and their children could
stay quiet enough upstairs,
perhaps the hungry Indians
would just raid their kitchens for
vittles* and leave the cabin
with no harm done.

REYNOLDS SMOKEHOUSE

The 1860s Reynolds smokehouse was moved to the village
to show how pioneers cured* their meat long ago.
After hogs were butchered, the meat was smoked
over a low fire for several days to make
hams or bacon for eating later.
I'm mighty grateful they didn't care for
smoked kitty cat in those days.

CAT TR🐾CK FACT:
Pioneers had no electricity for refrigeration, so they
preserved their food in many ways.

Meat would be smoked, dried, or salted.
Fruits and vegetables would be canned in glass jars or dried
over an open fire. Hard hot work like this added to the daily
list of chores for pioneer women and girls.

I'm the smokehouse kitty
Smellin' mighty yummy.
Hound dogs like to follow me with growlin' empty tummies.

Our blacksmith in the village still uses many authentic tools from the 1800s. The smithy heats the forge* with enough coal to turn an iron rod red-hot, then he hammers the iron into a nail, horseshoe, or farm tool atop his anvil.*

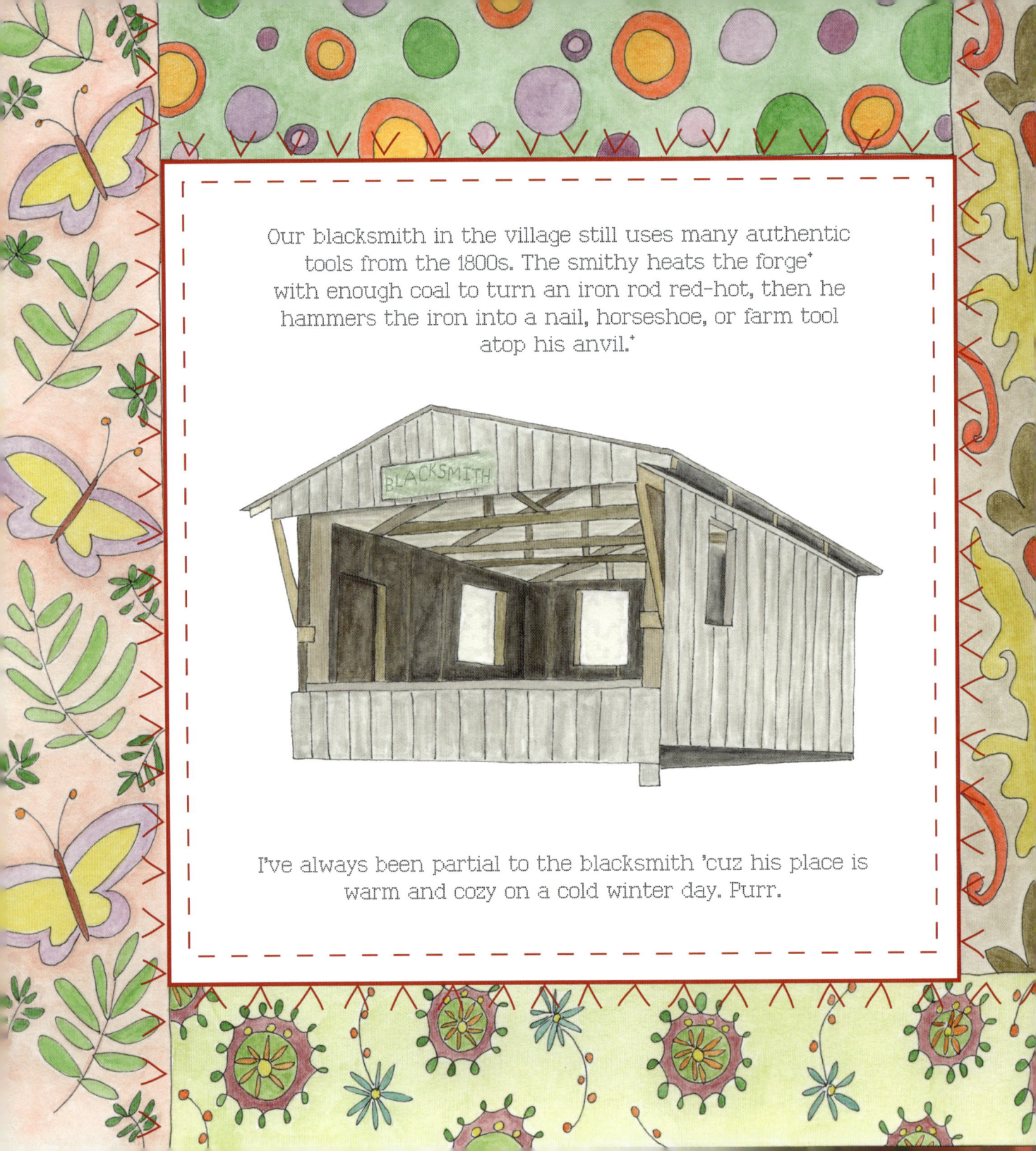

I've always been partial to the blacksmith 'cuz his place is warm and cozy on a cold winter day. Purr.

CAT TRACK FACT:
The blacksmith was one of the most valued people on the prairie because his tools and services were necessary for pioneer survival.

He was often one of the strongest men around from lifting his heavy sledgehammer all day long.

I'm the blacksmith kitty
Livin' by the fire,
A-hammering and bending horseshoes, nails, and wires.

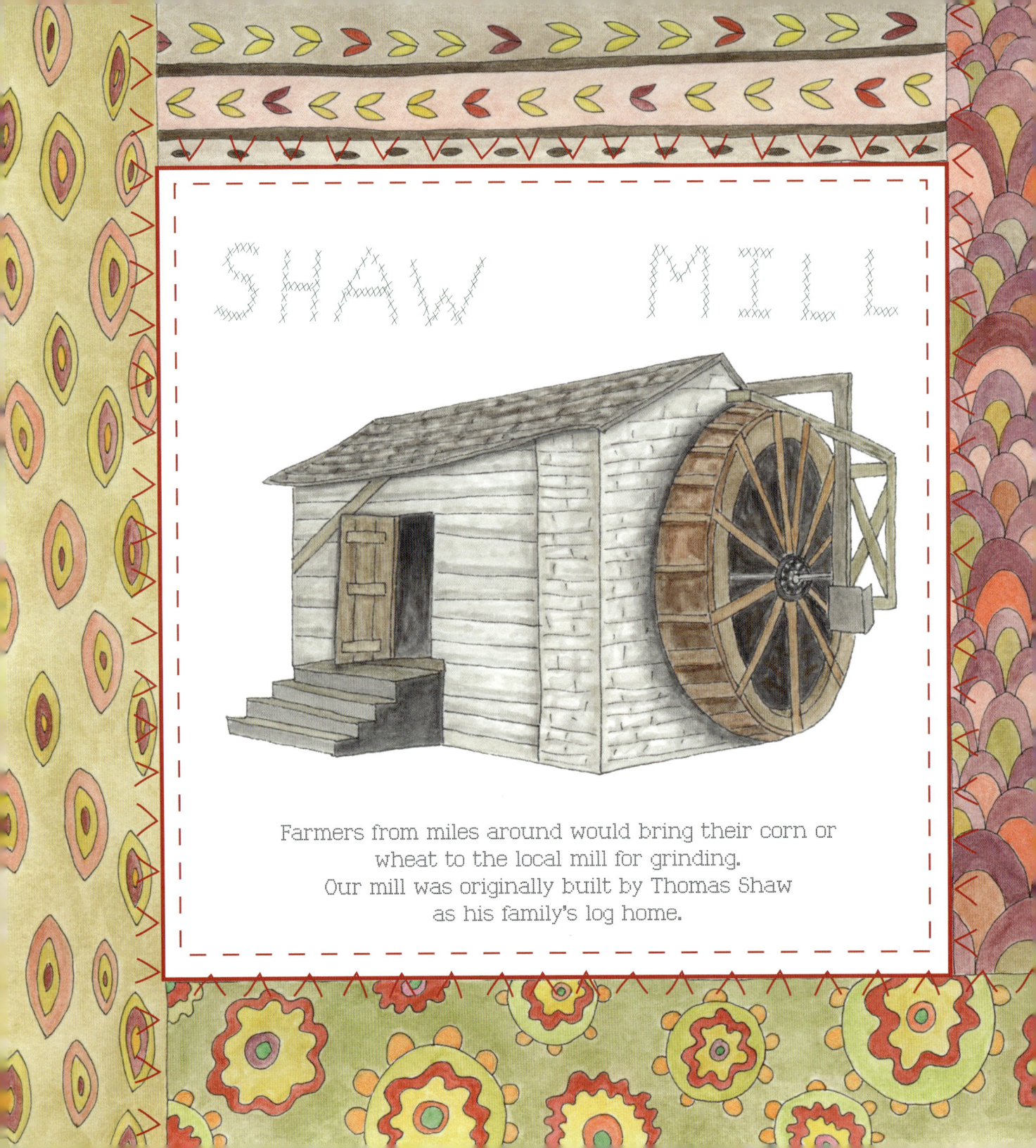

SHAW MILL

Farmers from miles around would bring their corn or
wheat to the local mill for grinding.
Our mill was originally built by Thomas Shaw
as his family's log home.

Folks here at the village rebuilt it into
a gristmill, an important part of pioneer life.
The 1860s Shaw Gristmill is water-powered by an outside
stream rushing down a flume* into buckets attached to
a wooden waterwheel.

Inside the log building,
a second wheel turns two stones that grind
dried corn into cornmeal.

I'm the Log Cabin Kitty
And I'm sittin' mighty pretty.
I live in a village from a long time ago.

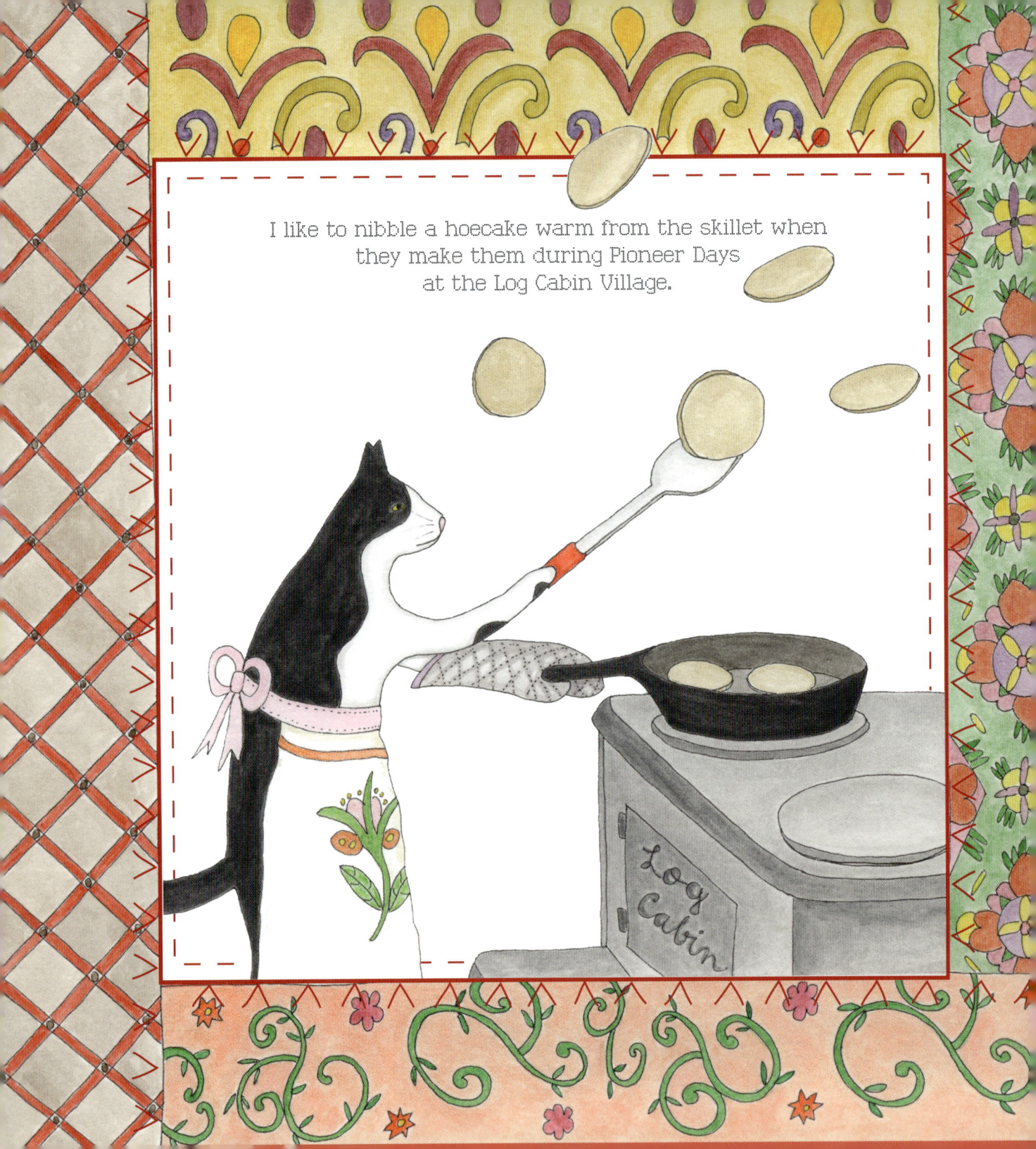

I like to nibble a hoecake warm from the skillet when they make them during Pioneer Days at the Log Cabin Village.

CAT TRACK FACT:
Grain-based foods were vital for hungry pioneer families.
Cornmeal was used to make rib-stickin' staples like
hush puppies and hoecakes.[+]

Here's a down-home recipe to try.

Hoecakes:
2 cups cornmeal
1/2 teaspoon salt
hot water

1/2 teaspoon baking powder
1 tablespoon melted butter

Combine dry ingredients. Add melted butter and enough
water to make a soft dough. Pat into cakes one-half inch
thick and cook on hot, buttered griddle until
brown, turning once.

Remember, always ask an adult to help you when cooking.

I love to rub my fur against the plants and sniff
the good smellin' scents in the herb garden.
The settlers knew which herbs to grow in
their gardens for medicine and food.

HERB CABIN

I'm the herb garden kitty
Smellin' fresh and sweet
With flowers in my fur and herbs beneath my feet.

Many a pioneer child was treated with horehound* for sore throats or chamomile* tea for coughs.

Because most illnesses happened during the bitter winter months when plants wouldn't grow, pioneers hung and dried herbs in their sheds for year-round use.
Mmmm, it smells so good here.

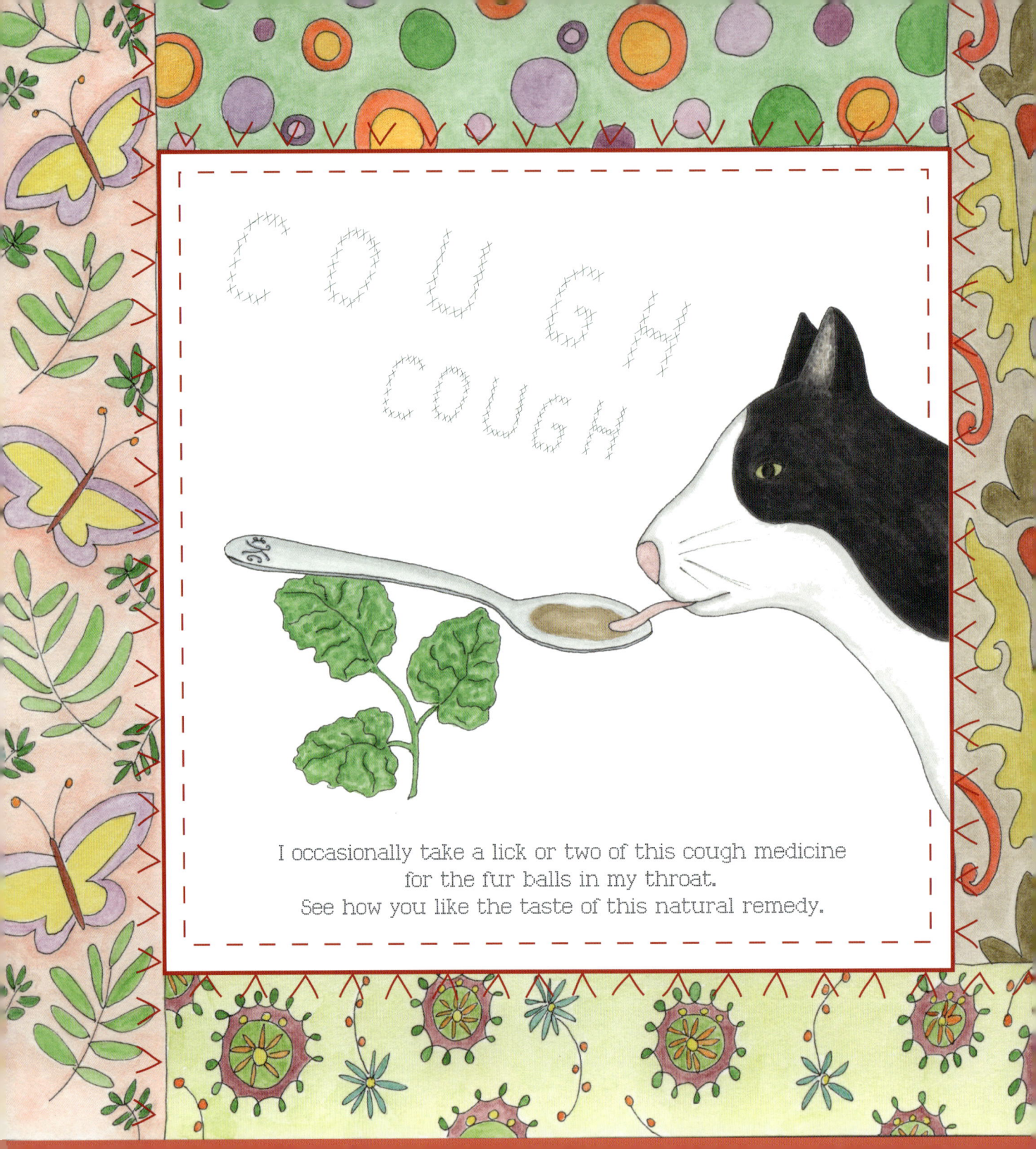

COUGH
COUGH

I occasionally take a lick or two of this cough medicine
for the fur balls in my throat.
See how you like the taste of this natural remedy.

CAT TRACK FACT:
Cough drops and syrup can be made from the downy
white leaves of the horehound plant found in most
pioneer herb gardens.

Horehound cough drops:

Boil several dozen horehound leaves in a small amount of
water. Strain the juice through cheesecloth.
Boil a small amount of sugar in enough water to dissolve
it and blend in the juice. Using a spoon, work the sugar
against the sides of the saucepan until thick and creamy.
Pour into a buttered pan and when cooled, cut
into squares and allow to dry.

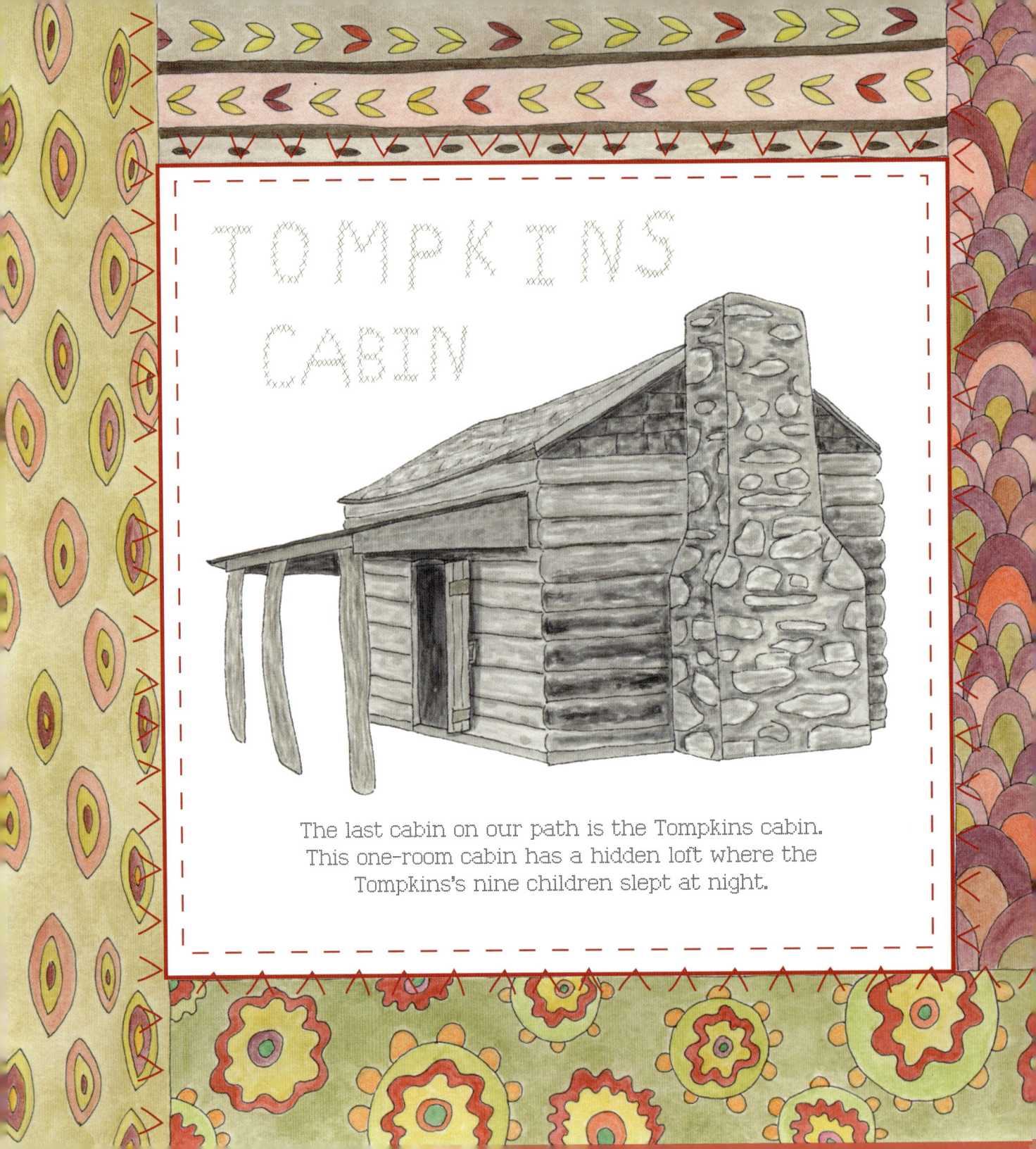

TOMPKINS CABIN

The last cabin on our path is the Tompkins cabin. This one-room cabin has a hidden loft where the Tompkins's nine children slept at night.

Just outside the cabin is our candle-dipping kettle.
Candles were a necessary source of light in log cabins.
Settlers would spin the cotton to make wicks, then
using a broach* they would dip up to twelve wicks
at a time in hot wax.
Mind you, it takes about a hundred dips to make
a single batch of candles.

I'm a candle-dippin' kitty
Working day and night
Making beeswax candles that'll fill a room with light.

CAT TRACK FACT:
Pioneer fathers would light a special candle called a
courtin" candle. The time it took the candle to burn
down to the bottom was all the time a young man
had to visit his lady friend that evening.

Better hurry, young feller.

Be sure to stop by on a crisp cool fall day and take a turn
dippin' in our copper kettle full of beeswax.

ME-—OUCH!

Hey, watch out—that's my tail not a candlewick.
Me-ouch, I could've been a kitty candle.

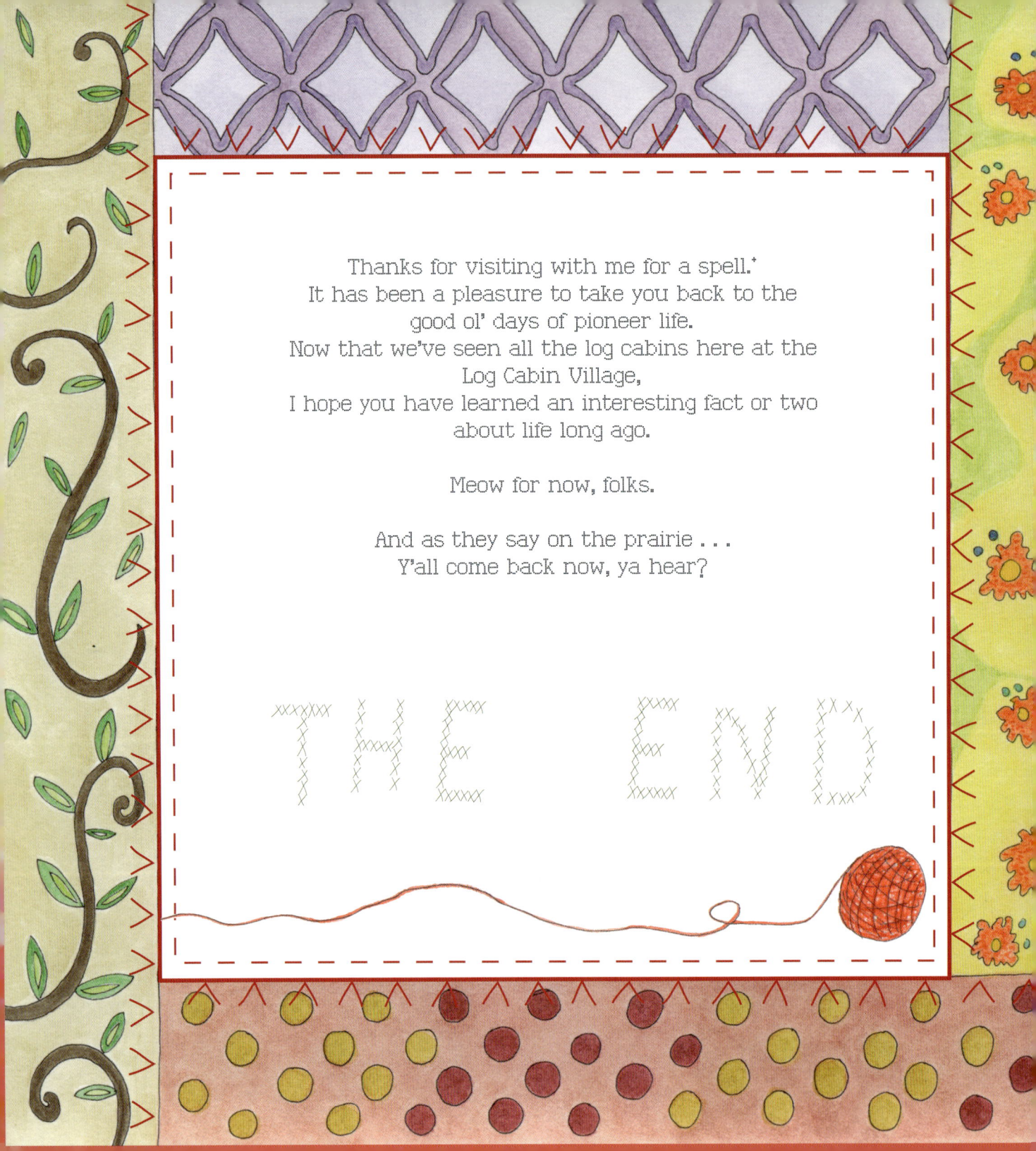

Thanks for visiting with me for a spell.
It has been a pleasure to take you back to the
good ol' days of pioneer life.
Now that we've seen all the log cabins here at the
Log Cabin Village,
I hope you have learned an interesting fact or two
about life long ago.

Meow for now, folks.

And as they say on the prairie . . .
Y'all come back now, ya hear?

THE   END

LOG CABIN

KITTY

I'm the Log Cabin Kitty
And I'm sittin' mighty pretty.
I live in a village from a long time ago.

GLOSSARY

anvil	a heavy iron block on which metal is shaped
broach	a wooden tool used to hold several cotton wicks
cipher	to compute arithmetically
chamomile	a strong scented herb used in tonics and teas
chink	to fill small cracks between logs
court	to gain the favor of someone
cure	to process meat for storage
dogtrot	a roofed open area connecting two buildings
dunce cap	a pointed cap worn by naughty students
flume	a channel for carrying water
forge	a forced air furnace
hewn	cut with an ax
horehound	a downy white-leafed herb
hoecake	a small cornmeal cake
homespun	loosely woven woolen or linen fabric

GLOSSARY

jacquard	a fabric with variegated weave
long johns	a one-piece suit worn under clothing for warmth
marm	slang for ma'am or madam
meander	to follow a winding course
mosey	to stroll
offspring	young children
passel	a large number
raid	to take by force or theft
reckon	to think or guess
settee	a sofa
scratch	to make by hand
spell	a turn at work
three Rs	reading, writing, and arithmetic
vittles	food supplies
yonder	a distance

LOG CABIN VILLAGE

FORT WORTH TEXAS

FOSTER CABIN

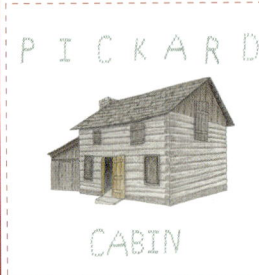

PICKARD

CABIN

SEELA

CABIN

PARKER CABIN

PARKER

DOGTROT

MARINE

SCHOOLHOUSE

KITTY CABIN

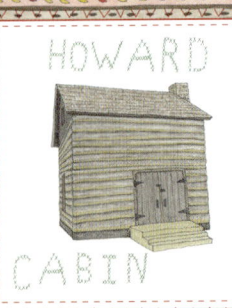

HOWARD

CABIN

REYNOLDS SMOKEHOUSE

BLACKSMITH

SHOP

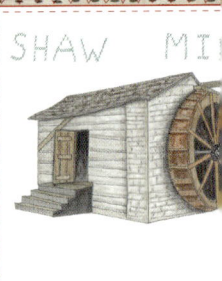

SHAW MILL

HERB CABIN

TOMPKINS CABIN

LOG CABIN

KITTY

LOG CABIN VILLAGE

FORT WORTH TEXAS

LOG CABIN
KITTY
FORT WORTH TEXAS

LOTS O'
CORN

STRONG
KITTY

Z Z Z

CLANG
CLANG

JACK AND JILL
WENT
UP A HILL

A STITCH
IN TIME

GO OD
KITTY

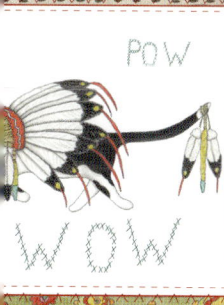
POW
WOW

GOOD
DOG

ABC's

CAT &
MOUSE

HOME

PEACE

ME OWWW!

KITTY
YUM
YUM

About the Author

DONNA RUBIN is a former first-grade teacher. A fifth generation Texan, Rubin now resides in Michigan with her family, including Pax, "the cutest dog in the world." *Log Cabin Kitty*, Rubin's first book, was inspired by sightings of the Log Cabin Village's friendly cats during nineteen years of field trips to the village with her students.

About the Illustrator

SUSAN J. HALBOWER has a degree in art from Kenyon College, but she learned to watercolor making books for her three young nephews. She is the owner of a line of cards and stationery, bow wow CARDS. Halbower previously illustrated *Smurglets Are Everywhere* (2010) for TCU Press.